An I Am Reading Latin Book

Who Loves Me?

Quis me amat?

"I Am Reading Latin" Series

This is one of a series of Latin books developed for ages 4–8. Other books include

What Will I Eat?
How Many Animals?
What Color Is It?

Check www.bolchazy.com for more information.
Recordings of these books also will be on the website.

Why learn Latin?

A short answer is that Latin
- develops a person's English
- provides a solid foundation for the acquisition of other languages
- connects us with the cultures of 57 nations on 4 continents
- provides us with cultural roots and a sense of identity
- enhances our career choices

Latin vocabulary forms the basis of 60% of the words in the English language, and it also forms the roots of the Spanish, French, and Italian languages. The very act of learning Latin serves to increase the mind's analytic processes, and an exposure to the Roman world constitutes a journey back to the roots of our own Western heritage. It's never too early to start learning Latin.

An I Am Reading Latin Book

Who Loves Me?

Quis me amat?

by **Marie Carducci Bolchazy**

translated by Mardah B. C. Weinfield
illustrated by Michelle Kathryn Fraczek
designed by Adam Phillip Velez

Bolchazy-Carducci Publishers, Inc.
Wauconda, Illinois USA

This publication was made possible by
PEGASUS LIMITED.

Printed in the United States of America
2003
by United Graphics

BOLCHAZY-CARDUCCI PUBLISHERS, INC.
1000 Brown Street, Unit 101
Wauconda, Illinois 60084 U.S.A.
www.bolchazy.com

ISBN: 0-86516-541-6

Library of Congress Cataloging-in-Publication Data

Bolchazy, Marie Carducci.
    Who loves me? = Quis me amat? / by Marie Carducci Bolchazy ; translated by Mardah
B.C. Weinfield ; illustrated by Michelle Kathryn Fraczek ; designed by Adam Phillip Velez.
    p. cm. — (An I am reading Latin book)
    Summary: Latin text and illustrations teach basic terms associated with family members,
then uses them in sentences. Includes translation, pronunciation guide, and glossary.
    ISBN 0-86516-541-6 (alk. paper)
    1. Latin language—Vocabulary—Juvenile literature. 2. Family—Juvenile literature. [1.
Food—Terminology. 2. Picture dictionaries, Latin. 3. Latin language materials—Bilingual.]
I. Title: Quis me amat. II. Fraczek, Michelle Kathryn, ill. III. Title. II. Series: Bolchazy,
Marie Carducci. I am reading Latin book.

PA2320.B656 2003
478.2'421—dc21

                                                                            2003040101

Haec est imago mei.

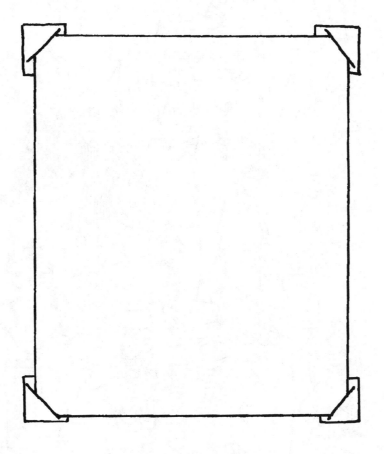

Haec est mea familia.

Mater

"Mihi opus est aliquo auxilio."

Pater

(tata omnium optimus)

murmur...
murmur...

5

Sorores

Frater

Avus

Avia

Avia

Patruus

Avunculus

Amita

Matertera

Consobrini

Quis me amat?

Mater me amat.

"Mama me tantopere amat!"

Pater me amat.

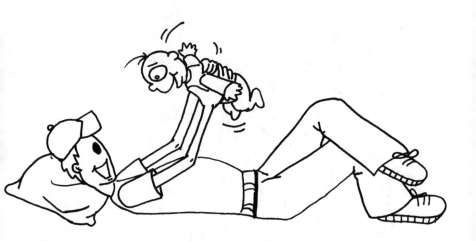

Sunt mihi duae sorores.

Sorores me amant...puto.

Frater me amat...

sed interdum

me vexat.

Avus me amat.

Aviae me amant.

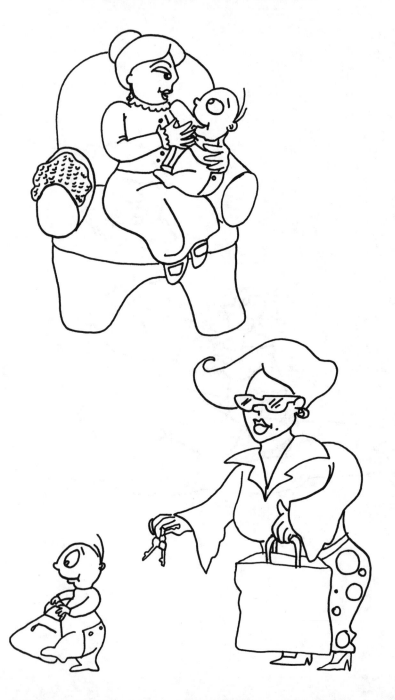

Patruus me amat.

Avunculus me amat.

Amita me amat.

Matertera me amat.

Mihi sex consobrini sunt.

Quinque e consobrinis
me amant,

sed unus credit me

molestum esse.

Deus me amat.

Sum amabilissimus.

Quem amo?

Ego quinque

e consobrinis amo,

sed sextus non semper

amicus est,

itaque eum semper
amare difficile est.

Amitam amo.

Materteram amo.

Patruum amo.

Avunculum amo.

Avias amo.

Avum amo.

Fratrem amo.

Eum me vexantem non animadverto.

Sororem maiorem amo.

Sororem minorem amo.

Patrem amo.

Matrem amo.

Deum amo.

Amare numquam me taedet.

Mea Familia

Mater

Pater

Avus

Aviae

Patruus

Avunculus

Amita

Matertera

Frater

Sorores

Consobrini

Translation

Page	Latin	English
Title	Quis me amat?	Who Loves Me?
1	Haec est imago mei.	This is a picture of me.
2	Haec est mea familia.	This is my family.
3	Mater	Mother
4	"Mihi opus est aliquo auxilio."	I need some help.
5	Pater	Father
	#I Tata	#1 Dad (on shirt)
	(tata omnium optimus)	(number one Dad)
	murmur...murmur...	mumble...mumble...
6	Sorores	Sisters
7	Frater	Brother
8	Avus	Grandfather
9	Avia	Grandmother
10	Avia	Grandmother
11	Patruus	Uncle (father's brother)
12	Avunculus	Uncle (mother's brother)
13	Amita	Aunt (father's sister)
14	Matertera	Aunt (mother's sister)
15	Consobrini	Cousins
16	Quis me amat?	Who loves me?
17	Mater me amat.	My mother loves me.
18	"Mama me tantopere amat!"	My mama loves me this much!
19	Pater me amat.	My father loves me.
20	Sunt mihi duae sorores.	I have two sisters.
21	Sorores me amant...puto.	My sisters love me...I think.
22	Frater me amat...	My brother loves me...
23–24	sed interdum me vexat.	but sometimes he teases me.
25	Avus me amat.	My grandfather loves me.
26	Aviae me amant.	My grandmothers love me.
27	Patruus me amat.	My uncle (father's brother) loves me.
28	Avunculus me amat.	My uncle (mother's brother) loves me.

29	Amita me amat.	My aunt (father's sister) loves me.
30	Matertera me amat.	My aunt (mother's sister) loves me.
31	Mihi sex consobrini sunt.	I have six cousins.
32	Quinque e consobrinis me amant,	Five of my cousins love me,
33	sed unus credit me molestum esse.	but one thinks I am a pest.
34	Deus me amat.	God loves me.
35	Sum amabilissimus.	I am very lovable.
36	Quem amo?	Whom do I love?
37	Ego quinque e consobrinis amo,	I love five of my cousins,
38	sed sextus non semper amicus est,	but the sixth is not always friendly,
39	itaque eum semper amare difficile est.	and so it is hard to love him all the time.
40	Amitam amo.	I love my aunt (father's sister).
41	Materteram amo.	I love my aunt (mother's sister).
42	Patruum amo.	I love my uncle (father's brother).
43	Avunculum amo.	I love my uncle (mother's brother).
44	Avias amo.	I love my grandmothers.
45	Avum amo.	I love my grandfather.
46	Fratrem amo.	I love my brother.
47	Eum me vexantem non animadverto.	I don't pay attention to his teasing (me).
48	Sororem maiorem amo.	I love my older sister.
49	Sororem minorem amo.	I love my younger sister.
	Fabulae	Fairy Tales (on book)
50	Patrem amo.	I love my father.
	#I Tata	#1 Dad (on shirt)
51	Matrem amo.	I love my mother.
52	Deum amo.	I love God.
53	Amare numquam me taedet.	It never tires me to love.
54	Mea Familia	My Family

Pronunciation Guide

Symbol	Key Words
ā	April, later, wait
ä	father, not
e	elephant, met, merry
ē	either, feet, honey
i	sit, mitten
ī	icy, kind, my
ō	over, most, load
ô	awful, paw, forget
o͞o	goose, ooze
u	umbrella, sun, mother
ʉ	serpent, surface
ə	a in comma
	e in supper
	i in Marilyn
	o in control
	u in circus

Note about Latin Word Endings

Consider the translations for *mother* in the following sentences:

Mother loves me.	*mater*
I love my mother.	*matrem*

These are just two of the ways to translate the word *mother* into Latin. Why are there different endings? Latin is an inflected language, which means that the ending of a word depends upon how the word is used in a sentence. In the examples shown above, *mother* is the subject of the sentence when the translation is *mater*, and the direct object of the sentence when the translation is *matrem*. Other sentence components, such as indirect object or object of a preposition, have different endings, too. In Latin, the ending identifies the usage.

Glossary

aliqui, aliqua, aliquod (ä′ lə kwē) some ALIQUOT

amabilis, -is, -e (ä mä′ bi lis) lovable

amicus, -a, -um (ä mē′ kəs) friendly AMITY, AMICABLE

amita, -ae (ä′ mi tə) aunt (father's sister)

amo, -are, -avi, -atum (ä′ mō) love, like AMOROUS

animadverto, -tere, -ti, -sum (ä ni mäd wär′ tō) pay attention to, notice

auxilium, -i (ôks i′ li əm) help AUXILIARY

avia, -ae (ä′ wi ə) grandmother

avunculus, -i (ä wun′ kə ləs) uncle (mother's brother) AVUNCULAR

avus, -i (ä′ wəs) grandfather

consobrinus, -i (kôn sō brē′ nəs) cousin

credo, -ere, -idi, -tum (kre′ dō) believe CREDIT, CREDIBLE, CREDIBILITY

Deus, -i (dā′ əs) God DEITY, DEIST, DEISM

difficilis, -is, -e (dif fi′ kə ləs) hard, difficult DIFFICULT, DIFFICULTY

duo, duae, duo (doo̅o̅′ ō) two DUO , DUET, DUAL, DEUCE, DUALISM

e, ex (ā, eks) out of, of

ego (e′ gō) I EGO, EGOTISM, EGOTISTICAL

est (est) is

et (et) and

eum (e′ əm) him (his)

fabula, -ae (fä′ boo̅o̅ lə) fable, fairy tale FABLE, FABULOUS, FABULIST

familia, -ae (fä mi′ li ə) family FAMILY, FAMILIAL, FAMILIAR, FAMILIARITY

frater, -tris (frä′ tär) brother FRATERNAL, FRATERNIZE, FRATERNITY,
FRATRICIDE

haec (hīk) this

imago, -inis (i mä′ gō) likeness, portrait IMAGE, IMAGERY, IMAGINE,
IMAGINARY, IMAGINATION

interdum (in tär′ dəm) sometimes

itaque (i′ tä kwe) and so

maior, -or, -us (mä′ yôr) elder MAJOR, MAJORITY

mama, -ae (mä′ mä) mommy

mater, -tris (mä′ tär) mother MATERNAL, MATERNITY, MATRIARCH,
MATRICIDE, MATRIMONY

matertera, -ae (mä tär′ te rə) aunt (mother's sister)

(mä) me ME

mei (me′ ē) of me

meus, -a, -um (mā′ əs) my

mihi (mē′ hē) to me, for me

minor, -or, -us (mi′ nôr) younger MINOR, MINORITY, MINUS, MINUSCULE

molestus, -a, -um (mō les′ təs) pesty MOLEST, MOLESTATION, MOLESTER

murmur, -is (mur′ mur) mumble MURMUR, MURMUROUS

non (nōn) not

numerus, -a, -um (noo′ me rəs) number NUMBER, NUMERAL, NUMERATOR, NUMEROLOGY

numquam (num′ kwäm) never

omnis, -e (ôm′ nis) all OMNIBUS, OMNIPOTENT, OMNIVORE

optimus, -a, -um (ôp′ ti məs) best OPTIMUM, OPTIMAL

opus est (ō′ pəs est) there is need OPUS, OPERA

pater, -tris (pä′ tār) father PATERNITY, PATERNAL, PATRIARCH, PATRICIDE, PATRICIAN

patruus, -i (pä′ troo əs) uncle (father's brother)

puto, -are, -avi, -atum (poo′ tō) think PUTATIVE

quem (kwem) whom

quinque (kwin′ kwā) five QUINT, QUINTUPLET, QUINTAIN, QUINTESSENCE, QUINTET, QUINTILLION

quis (kwis) who

sed (sed) but

semper (sem′ pār) always, at all times SEMPITERNAL, SEMPERVIRENT

sex (seks) six

sextus, -a, -um (seks′ təs) sixth SEXTET, SEXTUPLET, SEXTANT, SEXTAN, SEXTILE

soror, -is (sô′ rôr) sister SORORITY, SORORAL, SORORATE, SOROSIS, SORORICIDE

sum, esse, fui, futurus (sum) be, am, are

sunt (sunt) are, there are

taedet, -dere, -sum est (tī′ det) tire, irk TEDIUM, TEDIOUS

tantopere (tən tô′ pe re) so much TANTAMOUNT

tata, -ae (tä′ tä) daddy, grandpa

unus, -a, -um (oo′ nəs) one UNIT, UNITY, UNICYCLE, UNION, UNIQUE, UNIVERSE

vexans, -antis (weks′ änz) teasing, pestering VEX, VEXATIOUS, VEXATION, VEXED

vexo, -are, -avi, -atum (weks′ ō) tease, pester

Acknowledgements

We thank the officials of Wheeling High School in District 214 in Wheeling, Illinois for supporting the art in this book.

The illustrations in this book were arranged for by artist and teacher Thom Kapheim. We also thank Mary Pride, author of *Practical Home School Magazine*, for her suggestion that we develop Latin books for young children. Both Terence Tunberg and John Traupman reviewed the Latin for accuracy.

About the Author

Marie Carducci Bolchazy has a doctoral degree in education from the State University of New York at Albany and a masters degree, also in education, from Cornell University. She currently works full-time at Bolchazy-Carducci Publishers, owned by her husband and her. One of their specialties is Latin books. Customers frequently asked for Latin books for primary-level Latin, and the "I Am Reading Latin" series is her effort to fill that request.

About the Translator

Mardah B.C. Weinfield holds Master of Arts degrees in both Latin and Education. She has been studying and teaching Latin for over twenty years, most recently with her own sons, William and Samuel.

Note about the Illustrator

Michelle Kathryn Fraczek is a junior (2002–2003) at Wheeling High School and studies art with Thom Kapheim. She lives with her mom, dad and older sister. Her hobbies are drawing and painting, and she loves the Beatles. Michelle is also the illustrator of *What Will I Eat? (Quid Edam?)*